KONRAD MA

BOOK 1

LATE-ELEMENTARY PIANO SOLOS

200 Short Two-Part Canons

Opus 14, Nos. 1–100
EDITED BY MAURICE HINSON
INTRODUCTION BY HANS VON BÜLOW

PREFACE

Book 1 contains canons number 1 through number 100 representing the first half of *Two Hundred Short Two-Part Canons* by Konrad Max Kunz.

Konrad Max Kunz was born in Schwandorf, Germany, December 30, 1812, and died in Munich August 3, 1875. He studied in Munich with Hartmann Stuntz and was co-founder and conductor of the Munich Liedertafel, a male group gathered around a table for singing and refreshment. He composed many male quartets.

His *Two Hundred Short Two-Part Canons* has been very popular with beginning piano students since it first appeared. A canon is a strict form of counterpoint, the combination of two or more independent parts in a harmonious texture in which two or more voices must imitate exactly the same melody and rhythmic pattern in overlapping succession.

No interval larger than a fifth is used throughout these two hundred canons, which allows the student to keep his or her eyes on the musical score. Canonic writing for the keyboard requires both hands to automatically work independently of each other. In these pieces Kunz has given both hands the same thing to do, only earlier or later. Each canon is short—eight or sixteen measures—and rhythm, time, and keys have been varied.

Canonic writing, which is musical imitation in the strictest form, is the basis for eighteenth-century and much of the nineteenth-century keyboard repertoire. The student is advised to read through each part separately and then, when each part is mastered, play both parts together at a very slow tempo and then gradually increase the tempo.

Maurice Hinson

Project Manager: Gail Lew
Cover Design: Marco Brandão
Production Coordinator: Sharon Marlow

ABOUT THE EDITOR

Dr. Maurice Hinson is one of the world's most respected authorities on piano literature. He received the Lifetime Achievement Award from the Music Teachers National Association in 1994, an Outstanding Alumni Award from the University of Florida in 1990, and an Outstanding Alumni Award from the University of Michigan in the fall of 1995. Recently, he was awarded the Liszt Commemorative Medal by the Hungarian Government and the Medal of Excellence by the American Liszt Society for his research on the music of Franz Liszt. He is hailed as a specialist in American piano music, and some of his most recent articles appear in the *New Grove Dictionary of American Music*. He has given recitals, lectures, and master classes on five continents and in 48 states.

As senior professor of piano in the School of Church Music and Worship at the Southern Baptist Theological Seminary in Louisville, Kentucky, Dr. Hinson teaches piano, piano literature, and piano chamber music. He is the author of 11 books, including *Guide to the Pianist's Repertoire*; *The Piano in Chamber Ensemble*; *Music for Piano and Orchestra*; *The Pianist's Guide to Transcriptions, Arrangements, and Paraphrases*; *Music for More Than One Piano*; *The Pianist's Reference Guide*; *The Pianist's Bookshelf*; the *Vienna Urtext Piano Literature Guide*; and more than 100 articles. He is also the editor of more than 200 editions of piano music for various American and European publishers. Dr. Hinson is the founding editor of the *Journal of the American Liszt Society*, past editor for *The American Music Teacher*, and contributing editor for *The Piano Quarterly* and *Piano and Keyboard*. He records for Educo Records.

Dr. Hinson has been invited to serve on international piano competition juries, including the Gina Bachauer International Piano Competition, the University of Maryland Piano Competition, and the PTNA Young Artists Competition in Japan. A piano competition in his honor is sponsored by Southern Utah University.

Dr. Hinson received his B.A. degree from the University of Florida and his M.M. and D.M.A. degrees from the University of Michigan. He also studied at The Juilliard School and the University of Nancy, France (Conservatorie National).

PERFORMANCE NOTES

BY KONRAD MAX KUNZ

As soon as the beginner is able to play the following figure, he can use this collection of pieces to his advantage. He must be able to play the figure smoothly and connectedly in a number of transpositions, each to be repeated four times in succession, while carefully and continually being aware of the touch. His body, elbows, wrists, and fingers should be kept in proper positions, and at the same time he should count the beats (four to each measure) aloud and steadily.

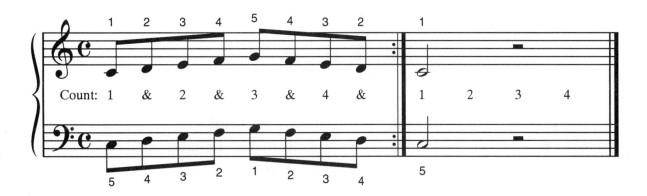

Speed is not necessary in these exercises. We have avoided:
1) The successive repetition of one and the same key, except in a slow movement or after a rest.
2) Employing the little finger and thumb on black keys, except from No. 182 onward.
3) The so-called dynamic signs of expression, such as f, p, crescendo, etc.
4) All doubled notes and grace notes; in due time these may be introduced by the teacher in their proper place.

On the other hand, the student should focus on tone production, connection of the tones *(legato),* and the acquirement of a *cantabile* (singing) style (for touch is to the pianist as attack is to the singer). He should also strive continually, from the outset, to acquire a clean, correct execution. The exercises are easy enough to accomplish this goal.

Every piano teacher who has taught beginners knows that any beginning is difficult. The great masters have left little or nothing for beginning students. The present work therefore aims, within its self-elected limits, to help fulfill this need. Nothing larger than the interval of a fifth is used in these pieces, so the student has no reason to look away from the music at the keys. The eye thus accustoms itself to the significance of the notation, mechanical playing by heart is avoided, and the student learns to "read." At the same time, care has been taken to offer no difficulty that the student is not able to master before becoming too familiar with his piece.

Later, of course, he will have to train his memory by memorizing daily a suitable number of the pieces that he has previously practiced.

The independence of the hands, i.e., the self-dependence of each, is to be attained most effectively, not by allowing one hand to act simply as the servant of the other but by giving them both the same thing to do, only earlier or later. To this end the form of the canon is best adapted, in which the students prepare their minds for the polyphonic style of the early masters. Finally, the pieces are all short because more developed movements easily overwhelm the capacity and patience of the beginning student. In order to avoid monotony, we have varied rhythm, time, and keys. Regarding the keys, hardly anything can be more wearisome, tiresome, stupefying, or indeed more cruel for teacher and student than being condemned to covering many large folio pages all in the key of C major. We have therefore employed all the usual keys and intentionally arranged them neither according to the circle of fifths nor according to their relationship as relative keys. Furthermore, the character of the melodies has also been varied by using the several tetrachords (with the addition, of course, of a note above or below when they have a range of a fifth) upon which the melodies are based. A melody, for example, that moves between the first and fifth degrees, will sound differently from one between the fifth and ninth, sixth and tenth, or seventh and eleventh of the same key. Changes of this kind, too, are introduced wherever possible. The imitations are for the most part in the octave but will be found quite frequently in other intervals. Some of them are inverted, and double-counterpoint in the octave is likewise employed. The different kinds of meter used are:

$$\frac{4}{2} \quad \frac{3}{2} \quad \frac{2}{2} \quad \frac{6}{4} \quad \frac{4}{4} \quad \frac{3}{4} \quad \frac{2}{4} \quad \frac{12}{8} \quad \frac{9}{8} \quad \frac{6}{8} \quad \frac{3}{8} \quad \frac{6}{16}$$

For advanced students, these canons may also be recommended both as sight-reading exercises and as materials for the study and practice of transposition. Many of them might also be used for singing exercises in attack and entrance, especially if suitable words are added.

More than 30 years ago, a series of 50 similar canons was published. A few years later, Royal Court Conductor Dr. Hans von Bülow encouraged the author to prepare a new edition. Without his encouragement, this edition would certainly not have been done. In preparing this new collection, the author discarded about 30 of his earlier canons. Among the present 200 pieces, very few of the earlier ones are to be found; the rest are newly written. This volume, therefore, appears as an entirely new work.

INTRODUCTION

BY HANS VON BÜLOW

Konrad Max Kunz, for his *Two Hundred Short Two-Part Canons,* deserves a high place of honor among writers of pedagogic piano literature—all the higher because not one of his contemporaries in this field happened to light on the clever idea of "combining the intellectual with the mechanical in technical studies, as applied to the early stages of development."

Although all enlightened music teachers may approve of this principle, its application to the first elementary exercises of beginners has been almost entirely neglected and, in my opinion, to great detriment. With no other instrument is it so important early to awaken and stimulate the faculties of feeling, thinking, and interpreting polyphonically as with the piano. The flexibility and fluency acquired by the fingers diligently practicing, for instance, the first five-finger exercises by Alois Schmitt, where the hands do simultaneous homophonic work, is gained, in most cases, only at the expense of musical intelligence. The diligent player involuntarily grows inattentive; lack of charm or interesting features in the task brings on absentmindedness and, finally, complete mental vacuity, with its inevitable result of unrhythmical playing. The player becomes a mere machine, forgetting that he should be the operator of a machine without whose care the latter, if it does stop, may lapse into irregular operation. Moreover, the natural coalescence and interdependence of right and left hands, a bondage from which the pianist cannot be too early emancipated, is materially promoted by exercises of this kind; an untrained ear controls only the right hand (soprano part) by which the left is taken in tow like a slave without will power of its own. These are, indeed, sad defects for which the acquisition of a certain mechanical dexterity provides no adequate solution. Such defects (the above-mentioned finger exercises of Schmitt, Bertini, Czerny, Köhler, etc.), can be remedied by the frequent use of and alternation with these exercises in canon form.

The essence or, indeed, the root of all polyphony is imitation: the canon. The simultaneous hearing of several musical parts has been proved to be physiologically impossible; only by training the intermediary reflective understanding does the faculty of successive apprehension become intensified to such a degree that the hearing appears to be simultaneous. In the simple strict canon, the faculty of recollection, which plays such an essential role in music, is set in motion, by which means the development of an aptitude for successive understanding is gradually facilitated and it assumes the force of a habit. Therefore, no firmer foundation for polyphonic comprehension can be laid than canonic exercises.

The present work also provides excellent preparation for J. S. Bach's *Inventions.* I feel that all public musical institutions as well as all competent private teachers should make this collection obligatory. I believe that Kunz's canonic studies are worthy of his reputation as an excellent musician—a reputation well founded on the high quality of his compositions.

QUESTIONS AND ANSWERS
FOR TEACHER AND STUDENT

BY MRS. FREDERICK INMAN (1883)

I recommend all students of these canons to play first the scale in which each canon is written before reading the new canon itself. It is then a good plan to play the scale a second time, putting it into the particular time of the canon, carrying out the rhythm as it is there carried out, whether in whole, half, or quarter beats. By this means the beginner will find both key and time of the new canon far less difficult than when attempting to play it without first becoming acquainted with its key and with its time.

T: What are our two chief guides in reading these canons?

S: The key signature and the time signature.

T: What does the time signature to the first eight canons mean?

S: It means that there are four beats in each measure, and one accent, or strong beat on count one.

T: In what key is the first canon written, and how many notes of the scale are used for it?

S: The key is C major. The notes are key-note or tonic; seventh or leading note; and second of the scale.

T: Are there any notes not belonging to the key?

S: There are no accidentals in Canon 1.

T: In Canon 2, there is an interval between two of the notes that is larger than the intervals found in Canon 1. What is it called?

S: In Canon 1 we find only major and minor 2nds (the interval from B to D). In Canon 2, the interval is a minor 3rd.

T: In Canon 3 there is an interval from F to A. What is it called?

S: The interval from F to A is a major 3rd.

T: What is the half note worth in Canon 7?

S: The half note is worth two counts in Canon 7.

T: What is the whole note worth in Canon 9, and what does the time signature there mean?

S: The whole note in Canon 9 is worth two beats. The time signature $\frac{3}{2}$ means that there are three beats in the measure, each beat the value of a half note.

T: In $\frac{3}{8}$ time, how many accents are there?

S: In simple triple meter, there is one accent on the first beat of each measure.

T: Why may we not count six to music written in simple triple time?

S: Because by doing so we would change it into compound duple time, which requires two accents.

T: On what degree of the scale does Canon 8 begin in the upper voice or part, and on what degree does it end in the lower part?

S: Canon 8, in the key of C major, begins on the fifth, or dominant, of the scale, in the upper voice, and ends on the same degree of the scale in the lower part.

T: In what key is Canon 12 written? What does the time signature mean, and where are the accents?

S: Canon 12 is in D minor, *relative* minor to F major, and *tonic* or *parallel* minor to D major. The time signature **C** means that there are four beats in the measure; it is in simple quadruple time, and the first and third beats are accented.

T: What is the difference between the key signature of D minor and that of D major?

S: The key signature of D minor is one flat, B♭, and that of D major is two sharps, F♯ and C♯.

T: What is the quarter note worth; what is the half note worth; and what is the eighth note worth in **C** time in Canon 12?

S: The quarter note is a one beat; the half note two beats; and the eighth note a half beat in ¢ time in Canon 12.

T: In Canon 12 and Canon 13, the measures are filled with four quarter notes. What is the time signature in both?

S: The time signature of Canon 12 and Canon 13 is *quadruple,* with four beats and two accents.

T: In Canon 12 there is a dot after some of the notes. What is a dot counted as? Is it a whole beat or only a part?

S: We count a dot as equal to half the time of the note that it follows. In Canon 12, following the quarter note (which is equal to one beat), the dot is equal only to half a beat.

T: In what key is Canon 13 written?

S: In the key of F major.

T: What is the quarter note worth in Canon 13?

S: The quarter note in Canon 13 is worth one beat.

T: Can the dot ever be a whole beat?

S: Yes; in Canon 86 in the last measure, the dot is a whole beat; because the time signature $\frac{6}{8}$ shows us that the quarter note there is two beats, the dot following it will therefore be one beat.

T: In Canon 13 there is an interval larger than a major 3rd. What is it called?

S: The interval in Canon 13 larger than a major 3rd is from F to the C below. It is called a perfect 4th.

T: In Canon 14, the note on the 3rd line in the treble clef is the interval of a 3rd from D on the 4th line, and in Canon 16 it is the same.

S: B and D have the same place on the staff in Canons 14 and 16; the interval between them is in both cases a 3rd, but the key signature in Canon 16 tells us that B there is lowered to B♭; therefore, if we know our key, we shall play a major 3rd wherever D follows B♭.

T: In Canon 15 there is an interval larger than a perfect 4th. What is it called?

S: The interval in Canon 15 larger than a perfect 4th is from D to A. It is called a perfect 5th.

T: In what key is Canon 16 written, and what intervals do you find in it?

S: In B♭ major. The intervals are minor 2nd, A to B♭, major 2nd, B♭ to C, and major 3rd, B♭ to D, in the higher part; also minor 3rd, A to C, perfect 4th, C to the G below, and B♭ to the F below, in the lower part.

T: What does the time signature of Canon 17 mean?

S: The time signature $\frac{3}{4}$ means that there will be three beats in every measure, each beat is worth a quarter note or 1/4 part of the whole note. The meter is simple triple time.

T: What does the time signature of Canon 19 mean?

S: The time signature $\frac{2}{4}$ means that there are two beats in each measure and that the beat will be the value of a quarter note. In $\frac{2}{4}$ time the meter is simple duple time.

T: What is an eighth note worth, and what is a sixteenth note worth in $\frac{2}{4}$ time?

S: In $\frac{2}{4}$ time, the eighth note is a half beat and the sixteenth note a quarter beat.

T: In what key is Canon 20 written, and what would the notes of the last measure make if written one over the other (as a block chord)?

S: Canon 20 is written in E major. E, G♯, and B, the notes of the last measure, make the tonic chord on the key-note or tonic of E major.

T: What is the meaning of the time signature of Canon 21? What is the meter, and how many accents does it have?

S: The time signature $\frac{6}{8}$ means that each measure will contain the value of six eighth notes. The meter is compound duple time, and there is an accent on beats 1 and 4.

T: Why may we not count 3 to music written in compound duple time?

S: Because we then change it into simple triple time, to which we may give only one accent.

T: How should all beginners count in $\frac{6}{8}$ time, unless the music is very rapid?

S: We should count 6 to compound duple time unless the pace is too rapid to allow for counting more than 2.

T: How much is a quarter note worth, how much is a half note, and how much is a sixteenth note in $\frac{6}{8}$ time?

S: The quarter note is worth two beats; the half note is worth four beats; and the sixteenth note is worth only a half beat in $\frac{6}{8}$ time.

T: In what key is Canon 21 written, and what chord could we make of its last three notes?

S: Canon 21 is written in A minor; A, C, and E, its last three notes, make the tonic chord on the tonic or key-note of A minor.

T: What single note represents the time value by which a whole measure of Canon 22 might be filled?

S: A whole note has a time value sufficient to fill the whole measure of Canon 22.

T: Is the dot ever worth less than half a beat?

S: Yes; in Canon 95, the dot is worth only a quarter beat. because the time is $\frac{3}{4}$ and the dot follows an eighth note, which the note there is only a half beat.

T: In Canon 62 there is a second dot used. What part of the beat is that?

S: Since the meter is duple and carried out by four quarter notes in the measure, the quarter note is only half a beat; the dot that follows an eighth note is, therefore, in such a case only an eighth of a beat; and as a second dot is worth but half the first, that second dot there is a sixteenth of a beat.

T: What would the value of an eighth note be in Canon 17?

S: An eighth note in the $\frac{3}{4}$ time of Canon 17 would have the value of only a half beat.

T: In what key is Canon 18 written, and what are the degrees of the scale used for it?

S: In the key of A minor. The degrees of the scale used are the tonic or key-note, A; the second, B; the leading tone, G$\sharp$; the fifth or dominant, E; and the sixth, F.

T: In Canons 34 and 43 there are sharps used that are not in the signature. Why are they used, and why is the G raised in Canon 18?

S: In those three canons the sharps not in the signatures are accidentals used in minor keys to show that the 7th has been raised for leading tones.

T: Why are we so careful to recognize the leading tones of all the keys?

S: Because they help us distinguish the minor from the major canons and also for the reason that the leading tone of a key is always the major 3rd of the chord on its dominant.

T: In Canon 58 the 7th of the scale of G$\sharp$ minor is already made sharp in the signature. What is, in that case, done to make it a leading tone?

S: F$\sharp$, the 7th, is raised half a tone and made double sharp ($\times$) to be a leading tone to G$\sharp$.

T: On which key of the piano is F$\times$ played?

S: On G natural.

T: On which key of the piano is the leading tone of F$\sharp$ minor played in Canon 34?

S: E$\sharp$, the leading tone of F$\sharp$ major and minor is played on the key of the piano called F$\natural$ (F natural).

T: In Canon 39, what is the meaning of $\frac{3}{8}$ as a time signature, and what is the meter?

S: The time signature $\frac{3}{8}$ means that there are three beats in the measure, each beat to be the value of an eighth note, or the eighth part of the whole note. The meter is called simple triple time.

T: What is the difference between the time signature of Canon 44 and that of Canon 48?

S: Both tell us there are six beats and two accents, and both are compound duple time; the difference is that the beat in Canon 48 has the value of a quarter note while that of Canon 44 has only the value of an eighth note.

T: Canon 44 is divided by a double bar into two strains; the notes of both strains are written in the compass of a 5th, but are they written in the compass of the same 5th?

S: No; the first strain of four measures is written in the compass of a 5th (from D to A), and the second strain of four measures is written in the compass of a 5th (from F to C).

T: There are two accidentals in Canon 44. Are they used as leading tones to the keys of D minor and F major?

S: Neither G$\sharp$ nor B$\natural$ can be leading tones of D minor or of F major.

T: To what keys, then, do the two accidentals of Canon 44 belong?

S: G♯ is the leading tone of A, the scale that begins on the dominant of D; and B♮ is the leading tone of C, the scale that begins on the dominant of F.

T: We found just now that in recognizing a leading tone we recognized also the major 3rd of a particular chord. Name that chord.

S: The *leading tone* of every scale, major or minor, is the *major 3rd of its own dominant chord.*

T: What chord notes can you find in Canon 44?

S: D, F, and A out of the first strain make the tonic chord of D minor; F, A, and C out of the second strain make the tonic chord of F major.

T: In what key is Canon 53 written, and how often does its leading tone occur?

S: Canon 53 is written in E minor; its leading tone, D♯, does not occur at all.

T: What does the time signature of Canon 53 mean, and what is the meter?

S: The time signature $\frac{12}{8}$ means that each measure will contain the value of 12 eighth notes. The meter is called compound quadruple time.

T: What should all beginners count to $\frac{12}{8}$ time, and how many accents does it have?

S: We should count 12 to $\frac{12}{8}$ time and accent beats 1, 4, 7, and 10 unless the time is too rapid to count more than four.

T: What key is Canon 58 written in, and what is its leading tone?

S: Canon 58 is in G♯ minor, relative to B major, and its leading tone is F✕ (F double sharp).

T: In Canon 69 B♭♭ is used. On which key of the piano is it played?

S: On the key called A♮ (A natural).

T: How many names has each white key of the piano and how many names has each black key?

S: Each white key has three names and each black key has two names.

T: In what key is Canon 85 written, and what is its leading tone?

S: Canon 85 is written in the key of C♯ major, and its leading tone is B♯.

T: On which key of the piano is B♯ played?

S: On the key called C♮ (C natural).

T: There is another major scale with a different name and with different notation from C♯ major, but the notes are played on the same keys of the keyboard. What is the name of that scale?

S: The scale that is played on the same keys of keyboard as that of C♯ major is written as D♭ major with flats, and its leading tone is C♮ (C natural).

T: What does the time signature of Canon 85 mean, and what is the meter?

S: The time signature $\frac{9}{8}$ means that each measure will contain the value of nine eighth notes. The meter is classified as compound triple time.

T: What should beginners count to $\frac{9}{8}$ time, and how is it accented?

S: We should count 9 to $\frac{9}{8}$ time and accent 1, 4, and 7 unless the pace is too rapid to count more than three.

T: In what key is Canon 127 written, and what is its leading tone?

S: Canon 127 is written in A♭ minor; its leading tone is G♮ (G natural).

T: What is the other minor key called that is played on the same keys of the piano as A♭ minor but has a different place on the staff?

S: The other minor key played on the same keys of the piano as that of A♭ minor is the key of G♯ minor, relative to B major, with five sharps.

T: In what key is Canon 134 written, and what is its leading tone?

S: Canon 134 is written in C♭ major, with seven flats; its leading tone is B♭.

T: What is the other major key that is played on the same keys of the piano as C♭ major but with different notation. What is its leading tone?

S: The other major key played on the same keys of the piano as C♭ major is written as B major, with five sharps; its leading tone is A♯.

T: In what key is Canon 135 written, and what is its leading tone?

S: Canon 135 is written in B♭ minor; its leading tone is A♮.

T: In what key is Canon 137 written, and what is its leading tone?

S: Canon 137 is written in the key of C minor; its leading tone is B♮.

T: What is the other key that has the same leading tone?

S: C major has the same leading tone as C minor.

T: What does the time signature of Canon 137 mean, and what is the meter?

S: The time signature ₁₆⁶ means that each measure will contain the value of six sixteenth notes, or sixteenth parts of the whole note. It is classified as compound duple time.

T: Could we find a whole note or half note in a measure of ₁₆⁶ time? Could we have a quarter note, and what is the value of an eighth note in this time?

S: We could not find a whole note or a half note in ₁₆⁶ time because the whole note would be worth 16 of these beats and the half note worth eight. We could have a quarter note, which would equal four beats, and the eighth note there equals two beats.

T: In what key is Canon 138 written, and how often does its leading tone occur?

S: Canon 138 is written in F minor; its leading tone, E♮, does not occur at all.

T: In what key is Canon 171 written; what is its leading tone; and how is it related to the key in which Canon 140 is written?

S: Canon 171 is written in A♯ minor, relative minor to C♯ major, in which Canon 140 is written.

T: In Canon 171 G double-sharp is used. On which key of the piano is it played?

S: On the key called A♮ (A natural).

T: Canon 69 is a good exercise for playing the white flats. Canon 171 is also good for playing the white sharps. But why can't

we call the leading tone in Canon 171 A♮ and write it so instead of writing and calling it G✕?

S: If we wrote G✕ as A♮, thinking to make it easier, our scale would have no seventh G, and G only is the seventh degree of A, whether G be ♭, ♮, ♯, ✕, or ♭♭; and A is the eighth degree of A, whether A be ♭, ♮, ♯, ✕, or ♭♭.

T: What kind of interval must there be in the scale, whether major or minor, *between the leading tone and the eighth*?

S: The interval *between the leading tone and the eighth* of every scale, whether major or (harmonic) minor, must be that of a minor 2nd, or diatonic half tone.

T: Is not the interval from A to A♯ a minor 2nd, since the two notes are separated by a half tone?

S: No, because A♮ is separated from A♯ only by a *chromatic* half tone; that is one that changes a pitch of a note but does not change its name or its place on the staff.

T: What is the interval from G✕ to A♯?

S: The interval is a minor 2nd because G✕ and A♯ are separated by a *diatonic* half tone; that is one that changes the name of a note and its place on the staff as well as its pitch.

T: Since all of these canons are written within the compass of a 5th, we do not find an interval in either part greater than a 5th; but what other intervals in the scale are there besides those to be found in these canons?

S: In every major and minor scale we find the major and minor 2nd; the major and minor 3rd; the perfect and the augmented 4th or tritone; the perfect and diminished 5th; the major and minor 6th; the major and minor 7th; the perfect 8va; and the major and minor 9th.

T: Are we able to see at once, by their places on the staff, whether the notes of these various intervals are separated from each other by a major, minor, perfect, or diminished interval as we sing or play them?

S: No, the staff shows no difference between a major, minor, perfect, augmented, or diminished interval; they look alike, as we noticed that the 3rds did in Canons 14 and 16.

T: What guides do we have to help us in naming and analyzing intervals correctly?

S: The knowledge of our keys and the position of the half tones in all of them, *for it is by the half tones of the key* that *all intervals* except the 8th are varied; some from major to minor, and others from perfect to augmented, and from perfect to diminished.

T: What is the name of the first degree of the scale?

S: The tonic.

T: What is the name of the fifth degree of the scale?

S: The dominant.

T: What is the name of the fourth degree of the scale?

S: The subdominant.

T: The chord on the tonic has been referred to, and also the chord on the dominant; is there a chord on the subdominant as well?

S: Yes, the tonic, dominant, and subdominant are the three principle bases of every key, and the three fundamental chords of the key are built upon them.

T: Konrad Kunz, in his Performance Notes, mentions the "relationship of keys." What does that mean? He mentions also "tetrachords." What are they?

S: Any key that we may be singing or playing in is related to five other keys: to that beginning on its dominant; to that beginning on its subdominant; to their relative minors; and to its own parallel minor. By tetrachord, as the word is now used, is meant *half of an octave scale.*

T: Have the tetrachords anything to do with the "relationship of keys"?

S: Yes, a great deal, because *each of the two halves* of every major diatonic octave scale is found—note for note—in another scale.

T: In what particular scales are the tetrachords found that belong to the key we are in?

S: The first four notes, or tetrachord, of the key we are in will be found in the second tetrachord, or half, of the scale beginning on its subdominant; and the second half, or tetrachord, of the key we are in will be found to be the first four notes, or tetrachord, of the scale beginning on its dominant.

T: We have found notes that make the tonic chord in some of the canons; but are there any chords written as such in these canons?

S: No, the canons are melodies.

T: Why are they called two-part canons?

S: Because the melody that is begun by one part is exactly imitated by the other part.

T: To what great subject does the study of scales, their bases, and their intervals lead us?

S: To the subject of chords, which are built on the bases with intervals taken from the scale we are in, and from its related scales.

T: May notes of related scales be used in melodies?

S: Yes, notes not belonging to the key are often used in melodies for ornament; and the leading tones and fourths of related keys for more than ornament.

T: Why will it help us when reading more difficult music, if we learn even in these canons, to see quickly the leading tones and fourths of the keys?

S: Because when we play the simplest chorales and hymns, we find that the accidentals there are mostly the leading tones and fourths of related keys put together in a chord that will change our key for a time.

T: Have these important leading tones and fourths anything to do with the two semitonic steps in each scale?

S: Yes, a great deal, because in every major scale the half tones have their fixed places between the third and fourth, and seventh and eighth, ascending and descending; therefore, we know that those important notes will move by half tones in their chords.

T: Can we sing or play the simplest written melody—as it is intended to sound—by merely knowing how to take all the notes of it *at their true distances, or intervals, from each other*?

S: No, we must also know how to sing or hold down all the notes of it *for their true length of time* before a melody can be sung or played as it is intended to sound.

T: If we accent by mistake the weak beats instead of the strong, will that alter the melody?

S: Yes, if the measure is intended to be regular, the exact place of the strong and weak beats is as important to the melody as the exact pitch of the higher or lower notes of it.

T: Is the regularity of the measure ever intentionally interrupted by syncopation in these canons?

S: Yes, in Canon 6 the first half of the strong beat is tied; and in Canon 7 the first half of the strong beat is silenced by a rest.

T: If we fail to notice the rests when singing or playing, will that alter the melody?

S: Yes, because the rests all have their different lengths; so, that silence as well as sound has its exact time, which must be carefully allowed for in the measure.

T: In Canons 49, 82, and 196 the strong beats are not interfered with, either by ties or by rests, and yet the accents are made irregular; how is it done?

S: The accents are displaced in many of the measures, by the first note being only half a beat, and the second note beginning with the other half beat and continuing into the next beat. By doing this, it means the accents are thrown on to half beats or whole beats that, in the regular order, would be weak or unaccented.

T: In Canons 80, 103, 155, 163, and others, the regularity of the measure is interrupted, though not by syncopation; how is it done?

S: In those canons the sign > *for emphasis* is put over many of the half beats and beats, which would in the regular measure be weak.

T: Why is it better for beginners to count six in $\frac{6}{8}$ time instead of only two; nine in $\frac{9}{8}$ time instead of only three; and twelve in $\frac{12}{8}$ time instead of only four?

S: Because the notes are apt to become unsteady when three or more are played under one beat. Also, when shorter notes for half beats or for quarter beats come in, as well as dots for eighths and double dots for sixteenths of the beat, all true rhythm in the melody is lost, unless 6, 9, and 12 are counted to $\frac{6}{8}$, $\frac{9}{8}$, and $\frac{12}{8}$ time by beginners.

T: In Canons 147 and 178, three notes in each measure must be played under one beat. Why is it so?

S: Because *triplets* are used; they are in each case half beats grouped together to be played in the time of two half beats, equal to one whole beat.

T: If we may neither *reduce* the number of beats for fear of losing the regularity of the time nor *increase* their number for fear of multiplying the accents, upon what are we to depend for true measure or rhythm when reading new music?

S: We must depend upon our seeing at once the exact proportion of our half beats, quarter beats, eighths, and sixteenths of the beat, *to the whole, and to each other,* and also upon our understanding the exact position of the regular accents as shown by the time signature.

T: Why is it not enough to know the exact proportion of the other notes to the whole note and to each other?

S: Because as we have seen, different time signatures give different values even to the whole note itself.

T: What does our study of the figured time signatures of the canons show us?

S: That we must be guided by the *upper* figure as to the number of beats in the measure, and by the *lower* figure as to the value of the beat note and the proportion of all shorter notes to it throughout the canon.

T: The upper figure of all compound *duple* time is six. What number is it that will go into six three times without a remainder?

S: Two will go into six three times without a remainder.

T: The upper figure of all compound *triple* time is 9. What number is it that will go into nine three times without a remainder?

S: Three will go into nine three times without a remainder.

T: The upper figure of all compound quadruple time is 12. What number is it that will go into 12 three times without a remainder?

S: Four will go into 12 three times without a remainder.

T: That makes it easy for us to remember the number of accents in each kind of *compound time.* But what does the expression *common time* mean?

S: Common time means *even* in distinction to the triple or *uneven*. Common time has an even number of beats, and in triple time their number is uneven.

T: We have several times seen the time signatures **C** and differently carried out in these canons as to the number of notes in the measure. What does Mr. Banister say about them in his textbook called *Music*?

S: Mr. Banister says: "In former times Triple Time was called *Perfect Time,* and was signified by a circle O, as the symbol of perfectness; and *Common Time,* as *Imperfect Time,* was signified by a semicircle, ⊂. The semicircle has assumed the form of **C**, which is the signature for *Quadruple Time (with two accents),* while ¢ time is *duple,* with *one* accent in the measure. Usually, moreover, ¢ time is more rapid in pace than **C** time." *

T: What does our study of the key signatures of the canons show us?

S: It shows us that we can never be guided by the key signature only in finding out what our key is; two keys, one major and one minor, being always indicated by one key signature.

T: What other knowledge must we then gain in order to be certain as to which of the keys we are playing in?

S: The knowledge of intervals. If we do not know the difference between a major and a minor 3rd, we cannot be certain of the mode of our key.

T: If the leading tone of a minor scale is always an accidental, won't that tell us?

S: No. Some of the minor canons do not have the leading tone in them at all.

T: It has been said that "it is by the half tones of the key that all the intervals except the *8va* are varied; some from major to minor, and others from perfect to diminished." What does Dr. Callcott say as to the influence of those half tones upon melody itself?

S: Dr. Callcott says: "as the whole doctrine of melody, or the tone of notes, must depend on a right conception of the two semitones and their places in the scale, great attention should be paid to this part of the subject by every musical student." **

T: Konrad Kunz, in his Performance Notes, recommends these canons for the use of advanced students in learning and practicing transpositions. What is transposition, and why are so many advanced players unable to transpose?

S: By finding out exactly what degrees of the scale are used in any of these canons, we are preparing to transpose; and by writing down the same degrees of some other scale in the same order as to time, and prefixing the new key signature and the old time signature, we can transpose any canon. But many advanced players do not know this.

T: In the first 11 canons there is no direction given as to the speed at which they are to be played. But how many differently worded directions do we find used for the others?

S: There are, in all, 19 differently worded Italian directions used in these canons to guide us as to their speed.

T: Has the beginner anything more to think of when trying to acquire what Konrad Max Kunz calls a "singing style" of playing, besides keeping true to the time signature, the key signature, the regular accent, syncopation, emphasis, accidentals, triplets, tied notes, dots, rests, and rates of speed?

S: Yes. There is the fingering and the touch to attend to also; both, if well studied, will help keep the tones and the rhythm "singing." There are the signs for repeating some of the strains; and one thing more to attend to, which is that in Canons 25, 32, 83, and others, the treble clef is used for both parts.

T: For all of these things, the student's eyes should never stray from the notation on the page; but what is the common error to which Mr. Kunz refers, how does he help us avoid it, and if the mind is used instead of only the ears and fingers in these canons, for what future work will it be preparing itself?

S: It is to avoid all excuses for looking at the hands that the compass of the fingering is

---

Music, by Henry C. Banister, pages 10 and 11, paragraph 24.
** *Musical Grammar* (1817), page 24, paragraph 55.

always limited to a 5th. To avoid discouragement from the difficulty of first beginning to read, the canons are all very short; double notes, ornamental notes, and many of the signs in musical notation are omitted altogether. Mr. Kunz would have us learn "to read," and he thinks that if the very common mechanical playing by heart is avoided from the start, then our minds will be prepared to understand the writings of the old masters.

T: Mr. von Bülow, in his Introduction, mentions "homophonic work of both hands" as destructive to musical intelligence; he would have the "polyphonic faculty" early awakened in players and adds that the use of the simple strict canon is the best foundation for "polyphonic apprehension"; Mr. Kunz also recommends his canons to be used as singing exercises with words below. How may the history of music make the meaning of these expressions clear even to beginners?

S: History shows us that *homophonic* music was music's earliest form; when we hear a single voice singing a melody, we are listening to homophonic music. When music first developed into its early *polyphonic* form in France and Flanders, two entirely different melodies were sung together, which led to the contrivance of imitation or canon. In the sixteenth century, since four canons would be sung together by eight voices, the voices would divide into pairs and some would reverse the melodies taken by the others.

T: What influence had the singing of music—in which so many parts had their own separate melodies—upon the progress of rhythm?

S: As the number of parts increased, the strictness in keeping the time of their movement must have increased also; but for that, the many unaccompanied voices could not have kept together.

T: How and when did the singing of these increasing numbers of different melodies together lead to the building up of chords, first to accompany the voices, and then the independent harmony, such as we find in the simplest chorales and hymns?

S: As Dr. Callott says in his *Grammar*: "Two or more melodies heard at the same time form harmony; and the different combinations of notes in harmony are termed chords." In the sixteenth century, organ accompaniment of chords for the voices began to be used; and later, chorales and hymns were written in which the voices moved at the same time instead of independently of each other as in the canons.

T: How are we to guard against playing by ear; and how can we best prepare for studying the harmony of the chorales and hymns?

S: By "reading" a new canon every day, guided by the time signature and key signature, and by finding out the leading tones, fourths, and tonic chords of all the keys.

T: Anthony Salieri, the Italian composer, lived and wrote when the chords had had time to become more perfect than when they first began to be used. Much had been written about the importance of tonic chords and triads before his day, but he wrote canons, and a living French professor—who has made it possible even for infants to observe harmony—has put words to some of them on purpose for children to sing. Her words for the first one—which begins on the notes of the tonic chord of the key—make a fit ending to our study of the two-part canons of Konrad Max Kunz; for even as such works grew out of single melody-singing, so should they in turn invite us to the study and practice of four-part harmony:

> *Viens; harmonie,
> Pour être unie
> l'art charmant,
> Touchant
> Du chant.

Mrs. Frederick Inman
Batheaston, Bath
June 23, 1883

Récréations Chorales. Vingt-quatre Canons composes par Antonio Salieri (1735–1825). Paroles de Mlle. L. Collin, professor of voice at the École Normale des Institutrices de la Seine, Paris, Librairie Ch. Delegrave.

200 Short Canons for the Pianoforte
Opus 14

KONRAD MAX KUNZ

*The composer intentionally left out tempo indications in canons 1-11.

**See performance notes on page 3 for a discussion of dynamic markings.

***The original cut time (₵) sign used throughout this collection has been changed to 𝐂 by the editor for easier reading.

ELM02009

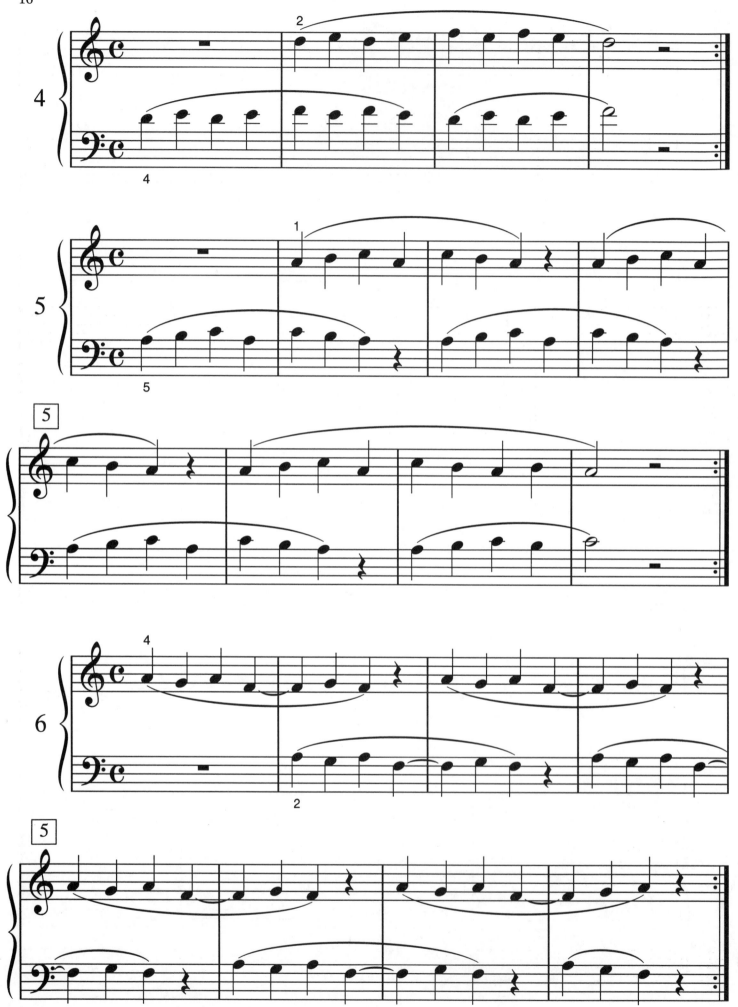

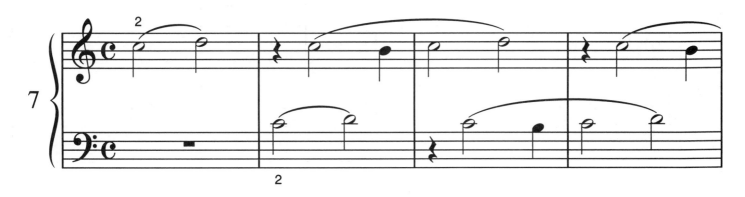

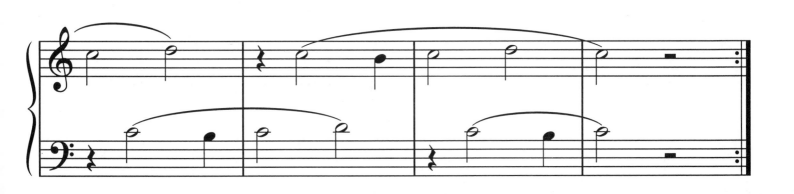

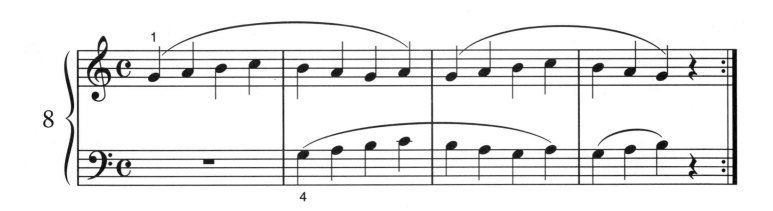

18

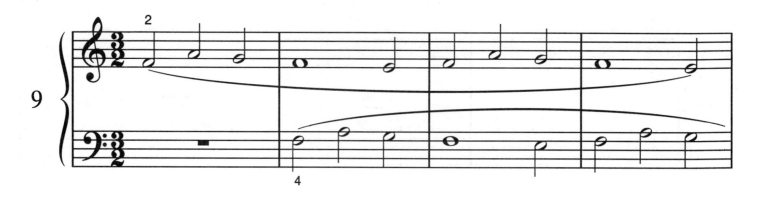

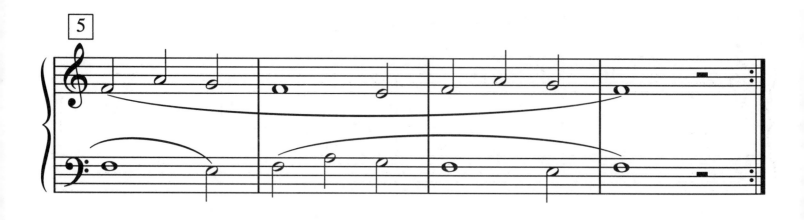

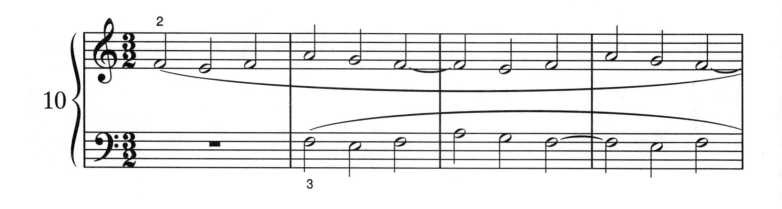

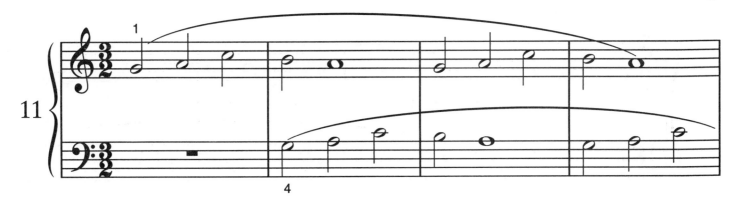

11

5

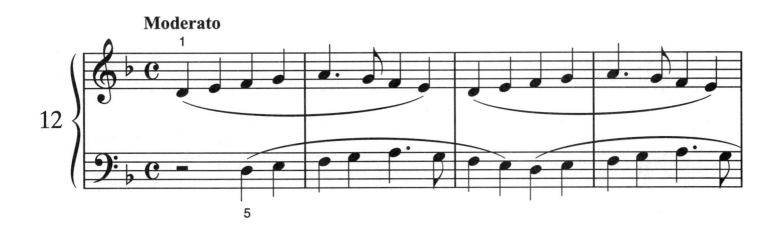

Moderato

12

5

Moderato

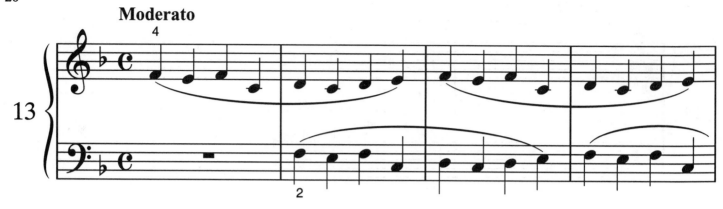

Allegretto*

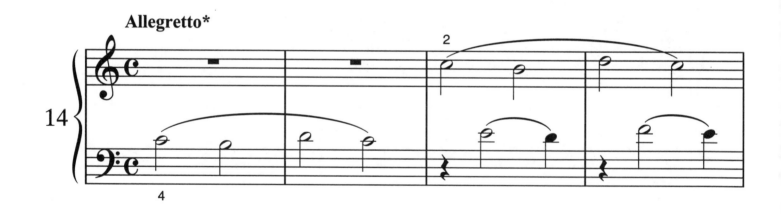

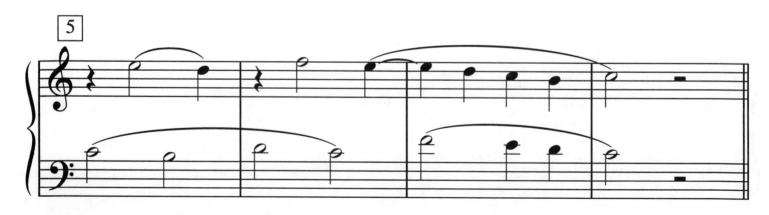

*Tempo indication is editorial.

ELM02009

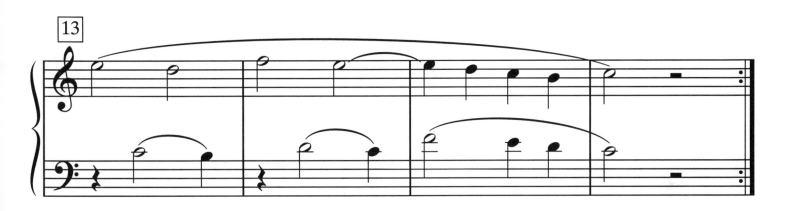

Allegro

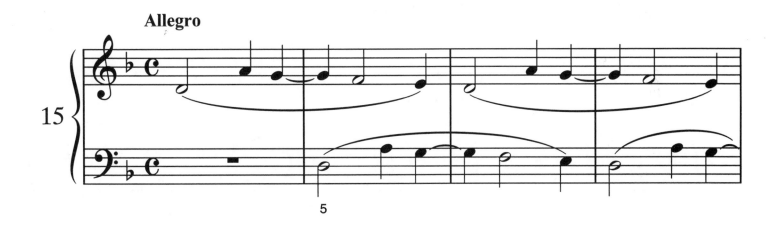

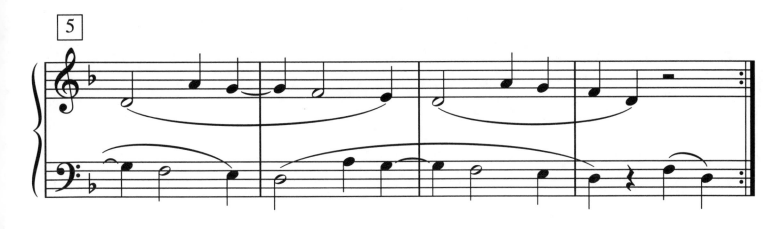

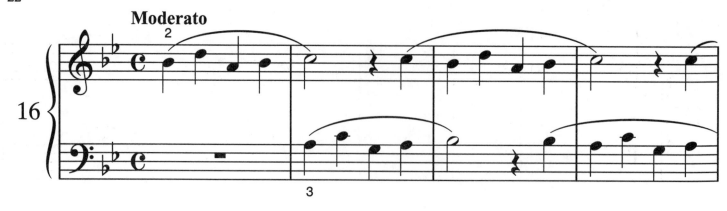

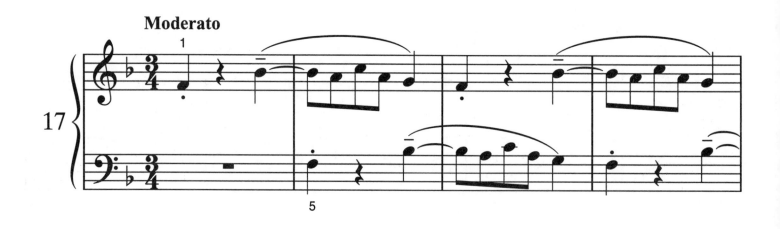

Allegretto

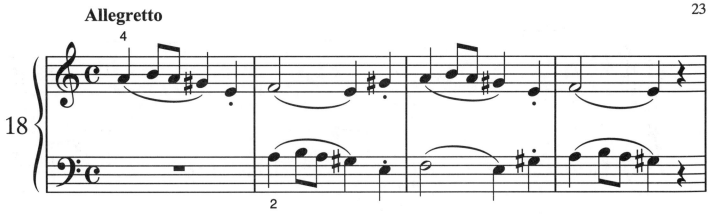

Allegro non troppo

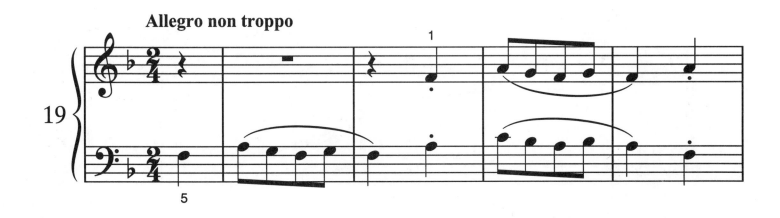

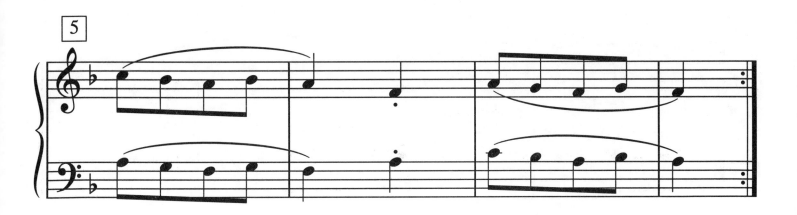

Con moto

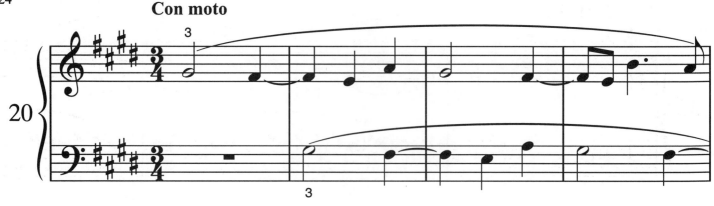

20

Andantino

21

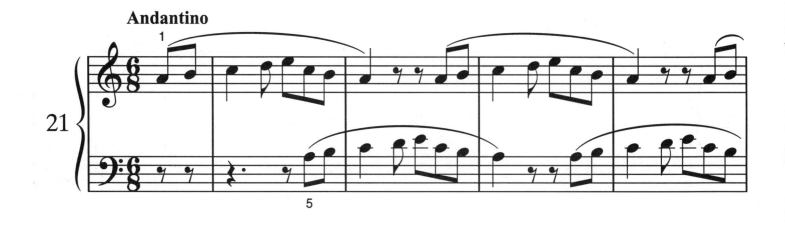

22

Moderato

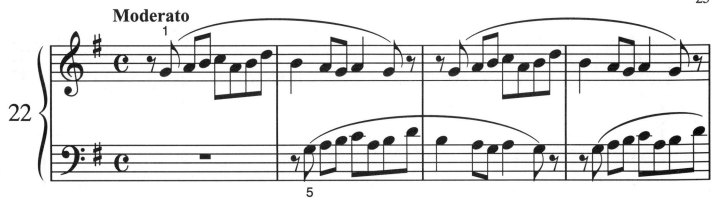

5

23

Andantino

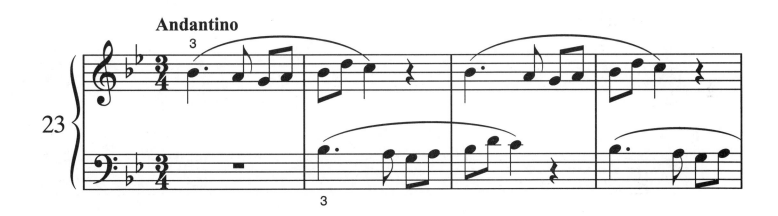

5

ELM02009

Andantino con moto

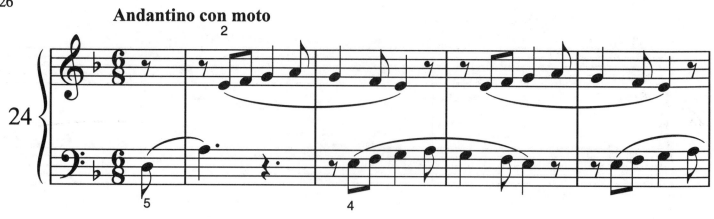

Allegro non troppo

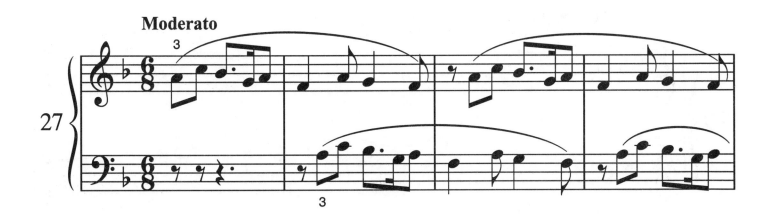

Moderato

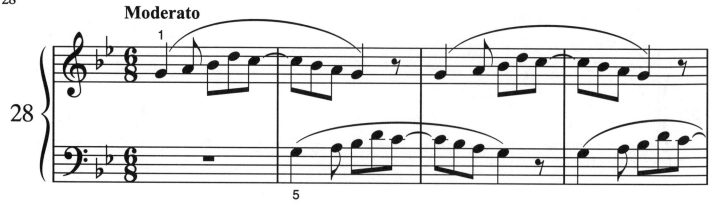

5

Allegretto

4

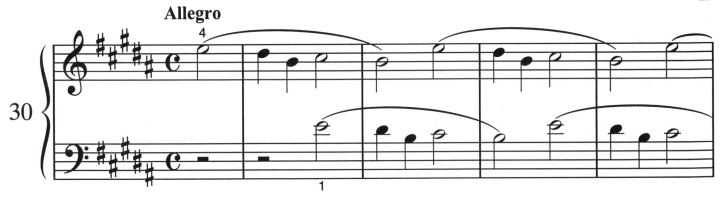

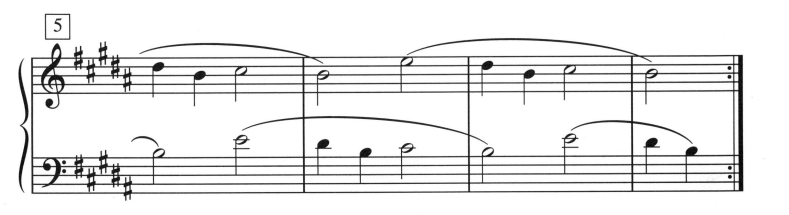

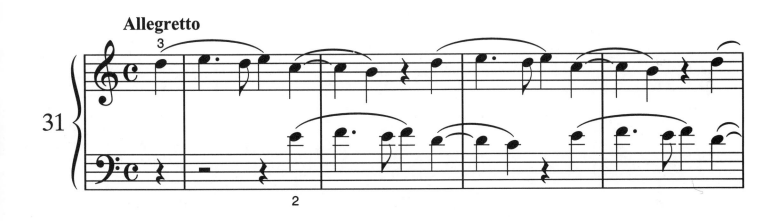

Allegro non troppo

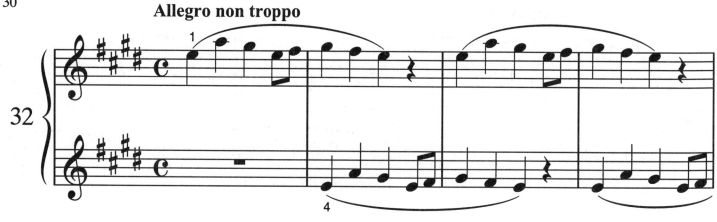

Allegro

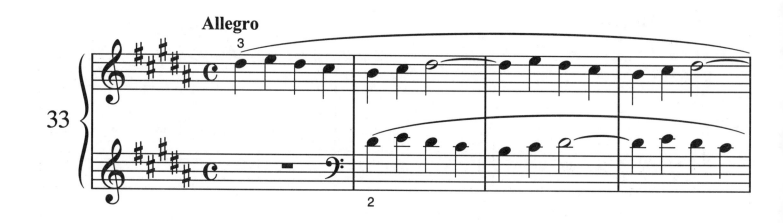

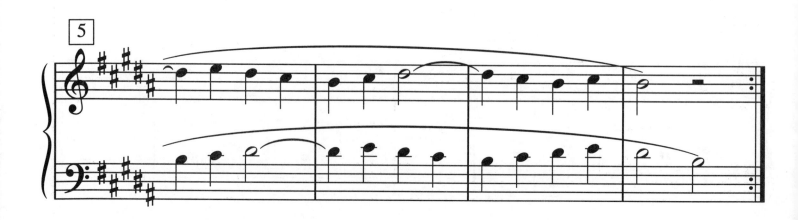

Allegretto*

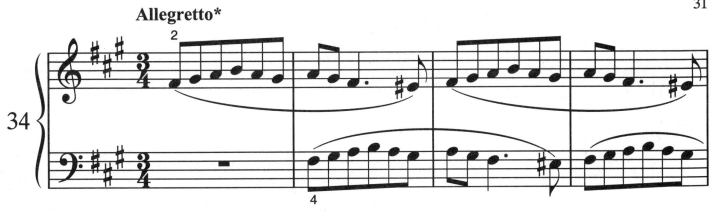

34

5

Allegro

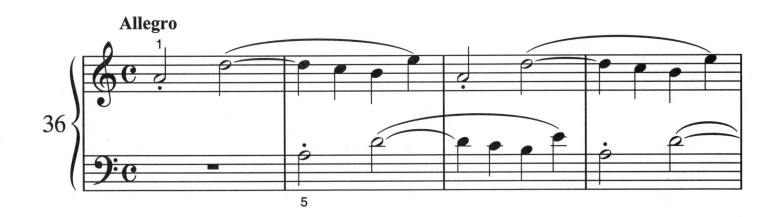

36

5

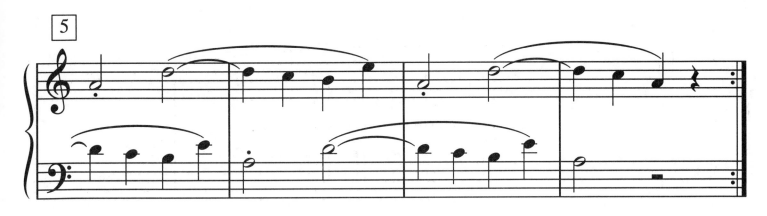

*Tempo indication is editorial.

ELM02009

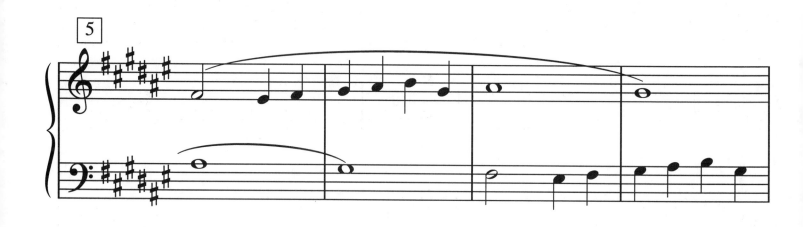

*Canon No. 35 was placed on page 32 to avoid awkward page turns.

39

40

Allegretto

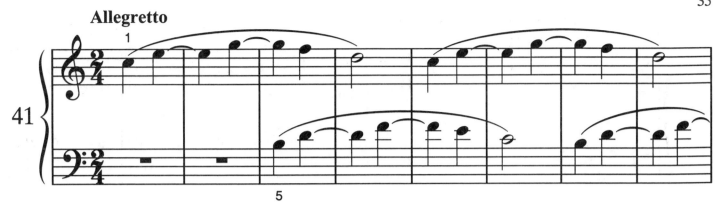

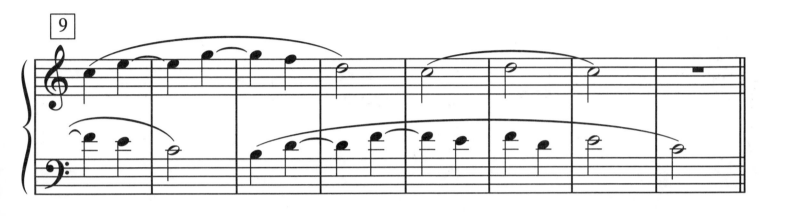

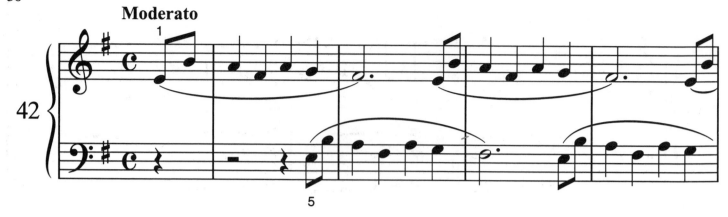

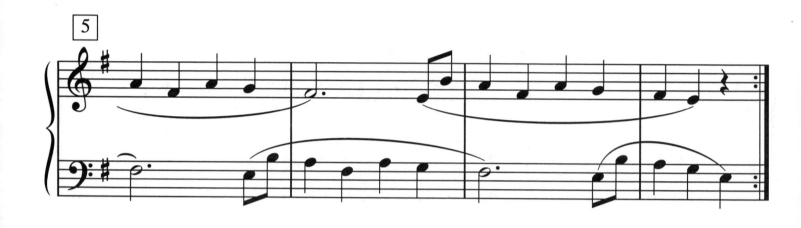

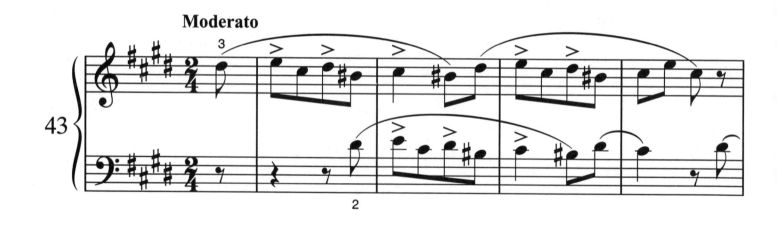

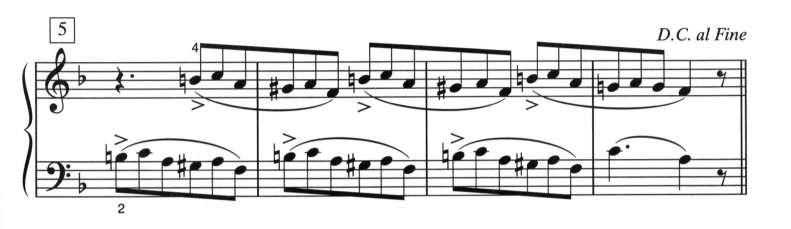

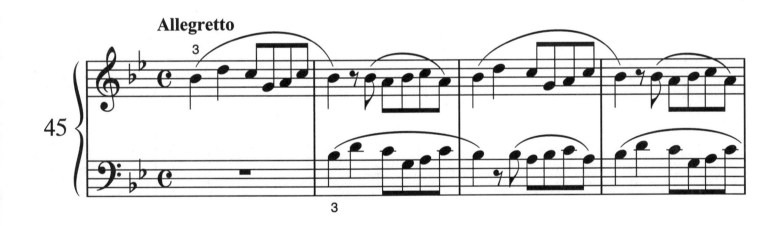

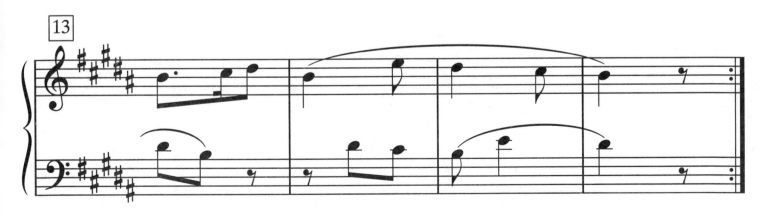

ELM02009

Allegro non troppo

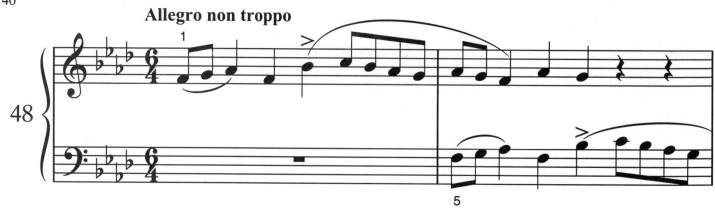

48

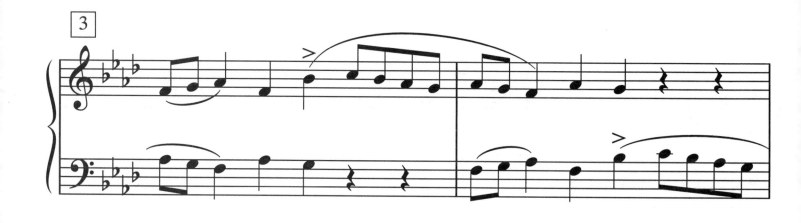

3

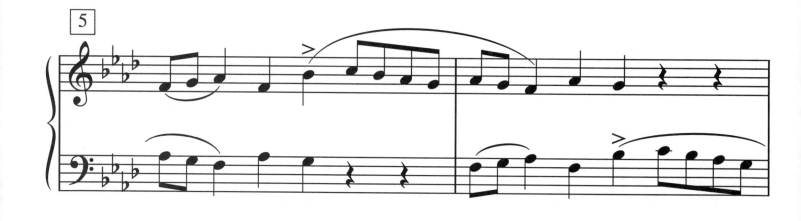

5

7

49

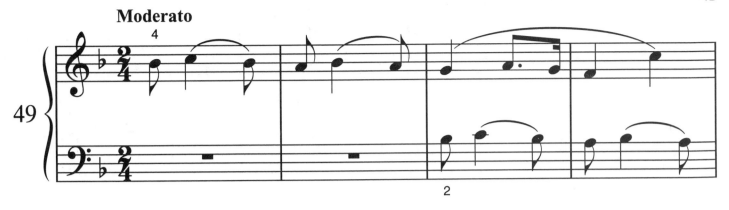

50

Allegro non troppo

5

Allegro

5

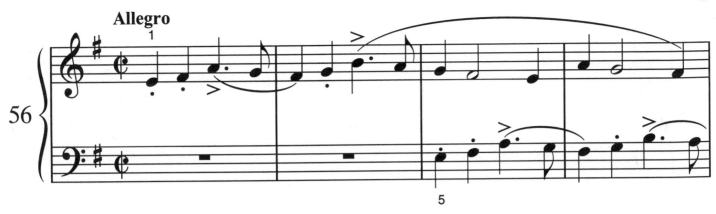

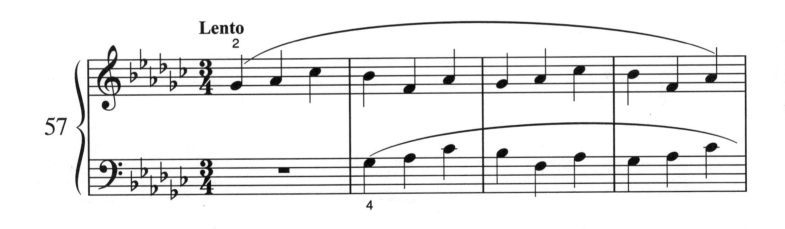

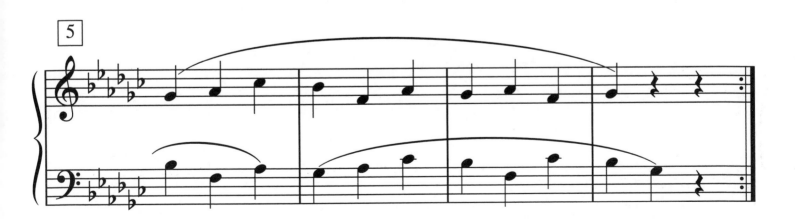

Andantino

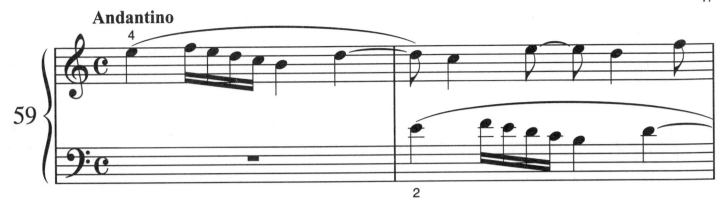

59

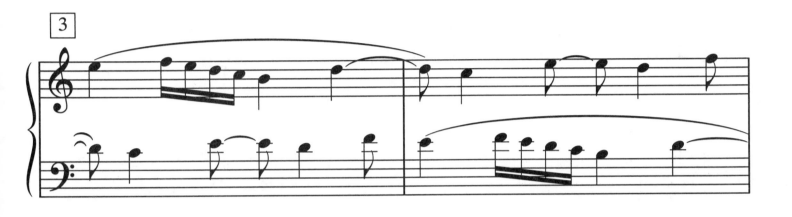

3

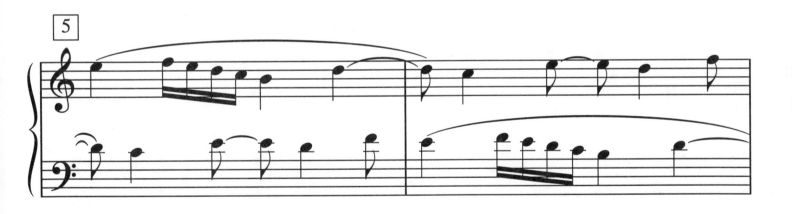

5

7

ELM02009

Andante

61

3

Allegro

62

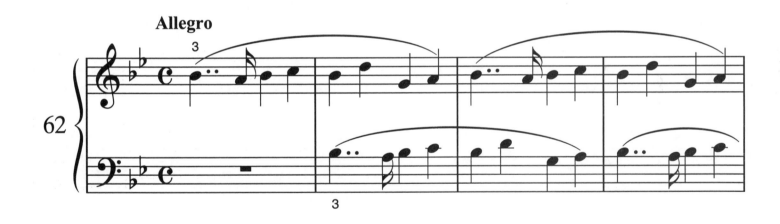

5

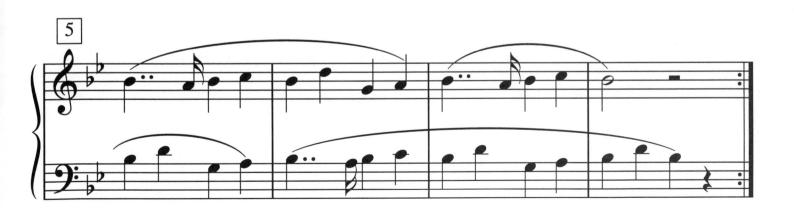

Allegretto

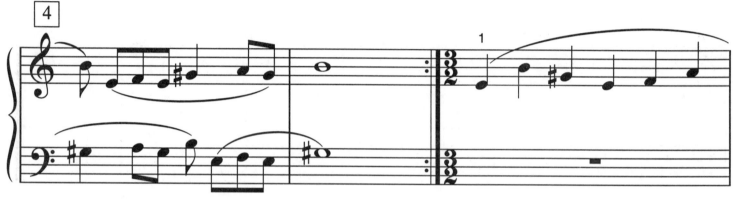

Allegretto

64

4

Moderato

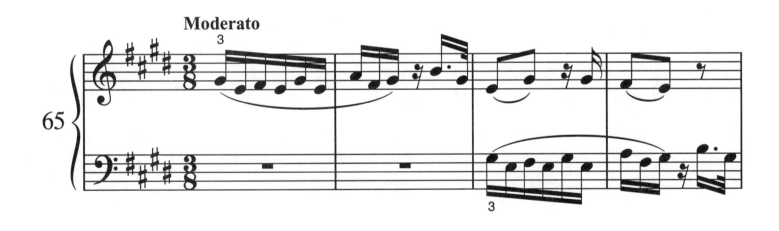

65

5

ELM02009

66

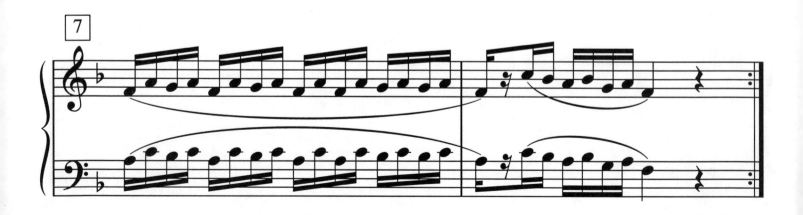

Allegretto

67

4

Allegretto

68

4

Poco lento

71

Andantino

72

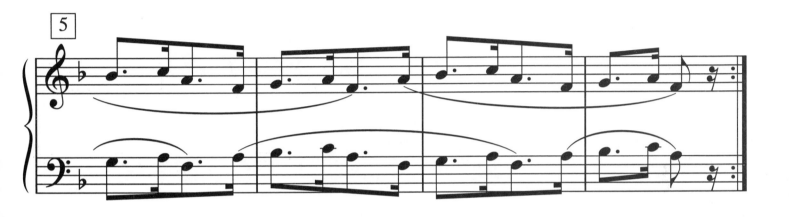

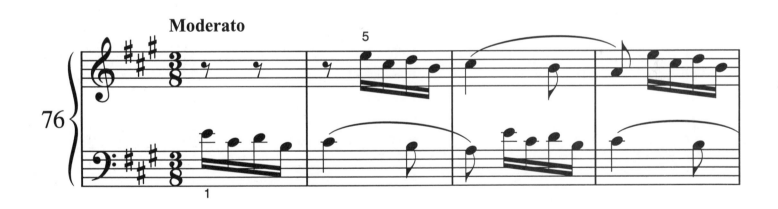

ELM02009

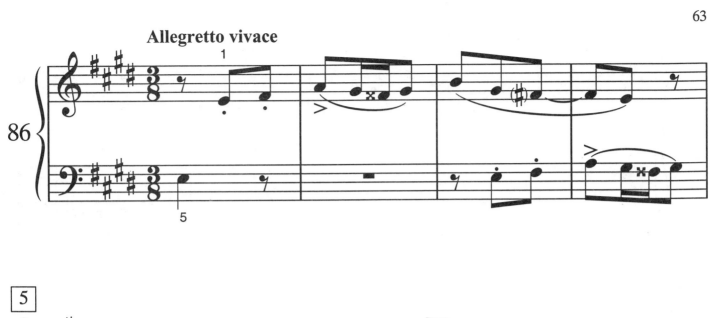

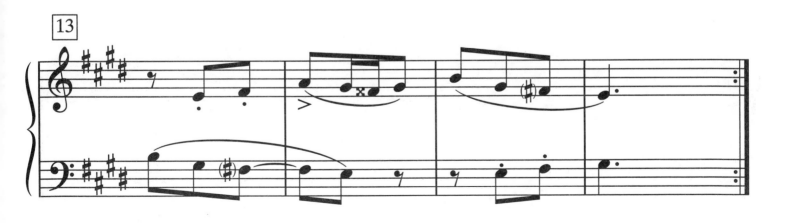

64

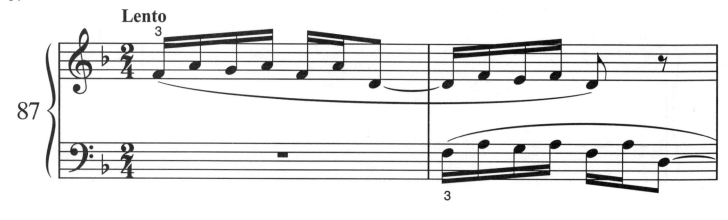

87

3

Moderato

88

5

ELM02009

Moderato

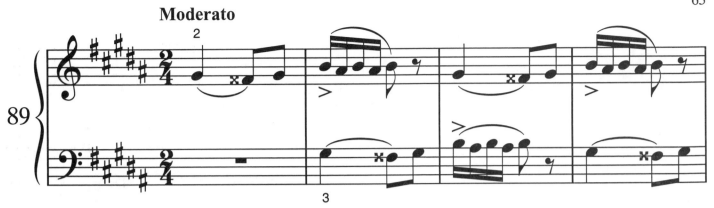

89

Con moto

90

66

93

Moderato

3

6

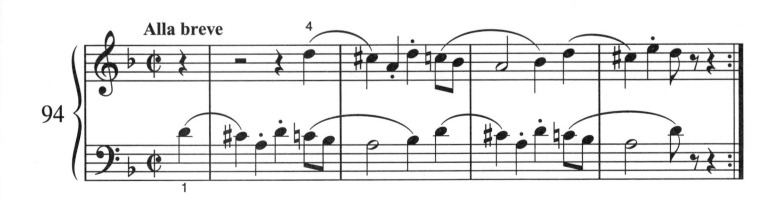

94

Alla breve

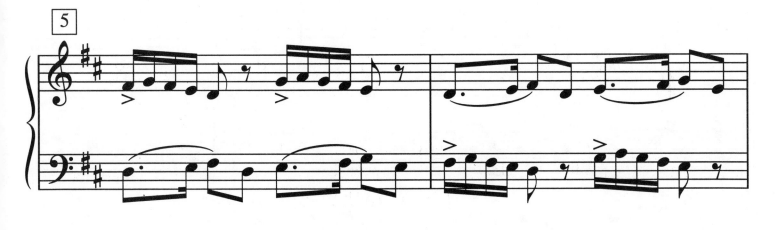

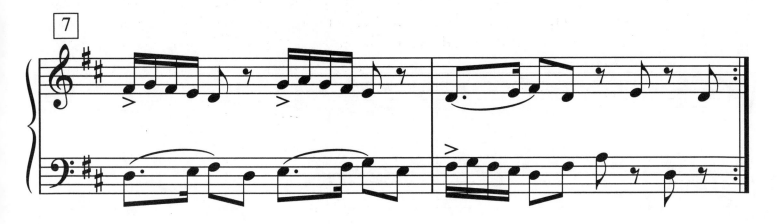

ELM02009

Moderato

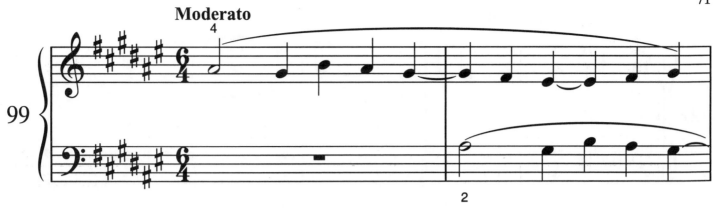

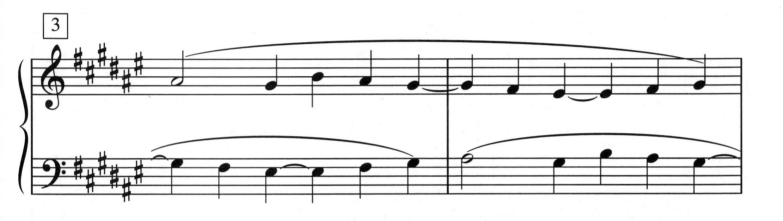

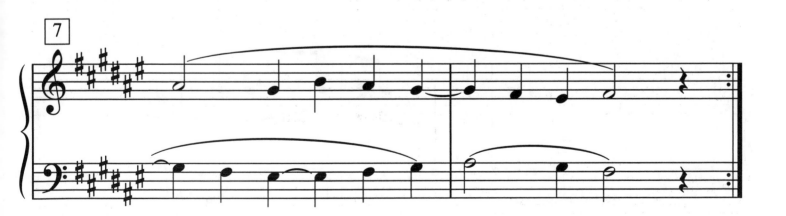

ELM02009

100